Crestwood House

SPORTS HEADLINERS

DAVID ROBINSON

CARL R. GREEN
ROXANNE FORD

CRESTWOOD HOUSE
NEW YORK
MAXWELL MACMILLAN CANADA
TORONTO
MAXWELL MACMILLAN INTERNATIONAL
NEW YORK   OXFORD   SINGAPORE   SYDNEY

Photo Credits:

AP—WIDE WORLD PHOTOS: Cover, 4, 10, 13, 14, 21, 22, 25, 26, 31, 34, 39, 42
THE ROBINSON GROUP: 8, 18

Cover design, text design, and production: William E. Frost Associates Ltd.

Library of Congress Cataloging-in-Publication Data

Green, Carl R.
  David Robinson/ by Carl R. Green and Roxanne
    Ford. p.   cm.—(Sports headliners)
    Includes bibliographical references and index.
    ISBN 0-89686-839-7
  Summary: A biography of basketball great David
  Robinson.
    1. Robinson, David, 1965 —Juvenile literature.
  2. Basketball players—United States—Biography—
  Juvenile literature. [1. Robinson, David, 1965–   .
  2. Basketball players.]   I. Ford, Roxanne. II. Title.
  III. Series.
  GV884.R615F57   1994
  796.323′092—dc20
  [B]   93-4976

CRESTWOOD HOUSE
MACMILLAN PUBLISHING COMPANY
866 Third Avenue
New York, NY 10022

MAXWELL MACMILLAN CANADA, INC.
1200 Eglinton Avenue East
Suite 200
Don Mills, Ontario M3C 3N1

Macmillan Publishing Company is part of the Maxwell Communication Group of Companies.

Printed in the United States of America
First edition

10   9   8   7   6   5   4   3   2   1

Contents

Few players are able to shoot the ball past basketball wonder David Robinson.

Chapter 1

A 40-Foot Miracle

On February 5, 1987, Halsey Field House at the U.S. Naval Academy buzzed with excitement. Local basketball fans had packed the stands to cheer for Midshipman David Robinson. The skyscraping 7-footer was the spark plug of the Navy basketball team. The Middies, the fans knew, would need all his skills against the Dukes, the team from James Madison University in Virginia.

After a slow first half, the Dukes opened a 39–26 lead early in the second half. The sudden surge sent the Middies a wakeup call. David led a charge that slowly closed the gap. With less than two minutes left, Navy pulled ahead, 70–68. That set the stage for the Dukes' Benny Gordon, who dropped in a long

three-point shot. The Navy fans looked at the clock and groaned. With only three seconds to play, the Dukes led by a point. David had won last week's game on a 17-foot jumper at the buzzer. Was it too much to ask him to do it again?

Middies coach Pete Herrmann called a time-out, but one second had ticked off the clock. His team had to move the ball the length of the court and score in just two seconds! Herrmann diagramed a play that he hoped would produce a miracle. David listened, shaking his head. Sure, Coach, he thought.

When play resumed, David took his place on the right wing, just over the center line. As Doug Wojcik waited to inbound the ball, David ran around a teammate's screen. An instant later he saw Wojcik's long pass sail over his head. David jumped high, tapped the ball away from a defender, and grabbed it. Off balance and falling forward, he threw the ball toward the basket. The shot looked wide to the left. No, it was on target! The ball hit the backboard and ripped through the net. The 40-foot miracle had turned defeat into victory, 73–71.

The crowd poured out of the stands. Some midshipmen hoisted David to their shoulders, all 7 feet 1 inch and 215 pounds of him. Laughing and shouting, the Middies paraded their hero around the court.

Later that night a reporter from *People* magazine talked to Coach Herrmann. The coach could think of only one word to describe David's game-winning shot. "Unbelievable," he said over and over.

Perhaps he shouldn't have been surprised. David Robinson thrives on challenges.

Chapter 2

A Student-Athlete Grows Up

David Maurice Robinson was born on August 6, 1965, in Key West, Florida. He almost did not live to celebrate his first birthday. Shortly after Ambrose and Freda Robinson brought their son home from the hospital, his head became wedged between the bed and the wall. He was turning blue when Freda found him. She quickly restored his breathing and rushed him back to the hospital. Doctors warned that the baby might have suffered brain damage.

The Robinsons picked up their son, said a prayer, and went on with their lives. The hardworking couple already had a daughter, two-year-old Kim. A second son, Chuck, was born six

David (left) and his younger brother, Chuck, are shown here in an old family photograph.

years later. David was still a toddler when the Navy transferred sonar technician Ambrose to Virginia.

Freda kept a close watch on her son. She stopped worrying about brain damage when he began reading at the age of three. When he started school, his teachers placed David in classes for gifted children. To shield their children from racial prejudice, the Robinsons raised them in a mixed neighborhood.

Sea duty kept Ambrose away for months at a time. Freda, who was a nurse, left notes reminding the kids to do their chores—and their homework. When David was in junior high, Ambrose grounded him for six weeks. His crime? He brought home a C on his report card. Even though they were often on their own, the Robinson children usually stayed out of trouble.

David earned good grades and learned electronics from his dad. He taught himself to play the piano by ear. By the age of nine, the young student-athlete was a terror on local baseball teams. A natural left-hander, he smashed home runs from both sides of the plate. In ninth grade David made the basketball team, but he did not enjoy the sport. A skinny 5 feet 7 inches, he played forward when he played at all.

In 1982, Ambrose retired from the Navy and found work as an engineer in Washington, D.C. David attended Osbourn Park High School in Manassas, Virginia, for his senior year. He had been doing a lot of growing. Coach Art Payne spotted the tall new kid and talked him into playing basketball. When the team's center went down with an injury, David moved in as the starter. His 6 feet 7 inch height and jumping ability made up for his lack of experience. Years later, Coach Payne said, "[David] probably improved more than any kid I ever coached. But at that point in his life, basketball didn't mean a lot to him."

David averaged 15 points and 12 **rebounds** per game. He won the team's Most Valuable Player (MVP) award and all-district and all-area honors. The college basketball scouts who saw him play called him a "project." They meant that he was a raw talent who needed lots of extra coaching.

Hard work and high test scores paid off for David in the spring of 1983. His family shared his delight when his appointment to the U.S. Naval Academy came through. Then, at the last minute, the doors almost slammed shut. The normal height limit for midshipmen is 6 feet 6 inches. David slipped in because the Navy accepts a few students who stand no more than 6 feet 8 inches. No one at Annapolis guessed that he wasn't through growing. By the time classes started, David measured 6 feet 9 inches.

Height and agility give David a clear advantage over many of his opponents.

Chapter 3

The Tallest Plebe

David chose the Naval Academy because he had grown up in a Navy family. Besides, he adds, "I needed a challenge. I was pretty lazy in high school…good grades came easy."

The academy, which is located at Annapolis, Maryland, gave David plenty of discipline. Mornings start at 7:30 with close-order drills. After breakfast the **plebes** (first-year midshipmen) march to classes in math, engineering, and computer science. The homework, David remembers, "varies from too much to way too much." Athletes had to hustle to squeeze in an hour or two for practice.

David's roommate, Carl ("Hootie") Liebert, was a basketball player. Hootie encouraged his new friend to join the team. David signed up, thinking basketball would be an easy way to earn a varsity letter. Sports also relieved the stress built up by the academy's fierce discipline and high classroom standards.

In gymnastics class, plebes were given three weeks to perfect their routines. Hootie expected David to flounder, but tumbling was a sport David had always enjoyed. He finished the course in a week—and earned an A. Soon afterward he broke his hand in a boxing class. The injury forced him to miss the season's first four basketball games.

When David returned, he rode the bench with the other substitute players. In a typical game he played 13 minutes and scored 7.6 points. No one called Navy's tallest plebe a star, but he did help the team win 24 games. It was the Middies' best record ever. Coach Paul Evans yelled at David when his center "spaced out" during games. "I was just trying to enjoy myself," David says. "Evans was playing these mind games to motivate me."

Perhaps the coach's tantrums paid off. During the summer of 1984 David played in a Washington, D.C., municipal league. His shooting improved, as did his footwork. Coaches said they had never seen a big man move with such grace and speed.

David was still growing. He stood 6 feet 11 inches and weighed 215 pounds when he returned to school in the fall. His added strength and improved ball handling made him a standout on offense and defense. In their third game the Middies beat American University, 84–68. David led the way with 29 points and 11 rebounds.

The Middies hit the early season jackpot at the Saluki Shootout in Illinois. David scored 31 points in one game and tossed in 37 the next night. In four games, all against top-flight teams, he averaged 28.8 points and 13 rebounds. Shootout officials named him the tournament's MVP. "Wow, I can play!" he told Hootie.

Navy ended the year with a 26–6 record. David averaged 23.6 points, 11.6 rebounds, and 4 **blocked shots** per game. His

David is shown here in a Naval Academy basketball photo.

total of 756 points broke an academy record. The East Coast Athletic Conference South named him its Player of the Year.

For the first time since 1960, Navy earned a berth in the **NCAA tournament**. After Navy beat Louisiana State in the first round, hopes for a national title ended with a loss to Maryland. The defeat was quickly forgiven at Annapolis. To the midshipmen, David and his teammates were heroes.

David earned several honors while playing for Navy. Here he is shown accepting the Los Angeles Athletic Club's John R. Wooden Award honoring the nation's top collegiate basketball student-athlete.

Chapter 4

A Big Decision

David was as amazed as anyone by his success. He looked back and said, "It was the first time I got an idea of what I could do." Friends began to ask him if he was going to play pro ball. David reminded them that academy graduates must serve five years of active duty. He could play pro ball—but not until 1992.

One solution was to transfer to another school. Coaches at major colleges called to tell him he would be welcome. A second escape route opened when he met with academy officials. The Navy, he was told, might shorten his tour of duty. Clearly, 7-footers were too tall to serve on submarines, surface ships, or planes.

David decided to stay at the Navy school. "The academy has

been good for me, and I want a chance to receive my degree from here," he said at last. "Something could happen, and you'd stop being a basketball player. You'll always benefit from being an officer." The news that David had put his country ahead of a big pro contract made him a national hero.

During the summer of 1985, David toured Europe with an all-star team. The pressure was intense, but his teammates never let up. He had to keep his mind on the game, David said, or "get absolutely killed." Back at the academy, Hootie noticed the change. "This year he is talking about how he can't wait to practice. I never heard him say that before," he told a writer.

The Middies started fast, winning seven of their first ten games. In their eleventh game, against the University of North Carolina at Wilmington, David racked up a **triple-double**. His 21 points, 14 rebounds, and 14 blocks set a Navy record. *Sports Illustrated* named him the nation's Player of the Week.

In a 70–53 win over Fairfield, David pulled down 25 rebounds. He also blocked 8 shots, made 2 **steals**, and scored 19 points. Sportscaster Al McGuire began calling him the Aircraft Carrier. The nickname was a tribute to the way he carried his team to victory.

David again earned East Coast Athletic Conference Player of the Year honors. When the NCAA tournament started, the Middies rolled over Tulsa, 87–58. Big Number 50's stats showed why: 30 points, 12 rebounds, and 5 blocked shots.

The win matched Navy against a strong Syracuse team. True to form, the Orangemen jumped into an early 17–8 lead. After a time-out, the Middies came roaring back to lead at halftime. In the second half, David sank two free throws, followed moments later by a **slam dunk**. Those four points gave Navy a lead it never lost. David finished with 35 points, 11 rebounds, and 7 blocks in the 97–85 victory. When he **fouled out** late in the game, the Syracuse fans gave him a standing ovation.

A narrow 71–70 win over Cleveland State set up a match with top-ranked Duke University. With David held in check by three defenders, the Middies' offense sagged. This time there was no second-half comeback. As the clock ticked down, the Blue Devil fans chanted, "A-ban-don ship! A-ban-don ship!" David said he and the Middies, upset by the 71–50 loss, had "played like wimps."

David's 1985–1986 season stats helped ease the pain. He led the nation in rebounding and ranked fourteenth in scoring, with a 22.7 average. More impressive were his three NCAA records: most shots blocked in a game (14), most shots blocked in a season (207), and most shots blocked in a career (372). And he still had a year to play.

When he's not playing basketball, David enjoys playing his piano and saxophone.

Chapter 5

Good News and Bad

David juggled basketball and naval duties during the summer of 1986. First he won a spot on the U.S. national basketball team. Then he boarded an aircraft carrier for two weeks of training. In June he flew to Europe with the U.S. team for the World Basketball Championships.

The United States and the Soviet Union swept into the finals without losing a game. David was at his best in the medal game between the two countries, holding 7 foot 2 inch Arvidas Sabonis of the Soviet team to 16 points. The surprise star of the game was 5 foot 3 inch Tyrone Bogues. The Soviets could not cope with the lightning-quick guard, who ran off with 10 steals. Thanks to David and his tiny partner, the United States won the gold, 87–85.

In August the Navy sent David to Quantico, Virginia. There he participated in some war games before returning to Annapolis for his last year. Despite his busy schedule, David reached out to others whenever he could. He spent time with a local youngster he had taken under his wing as his little brother. When invited, he also visited schools to talk to kids about staying off drugs.

Could the basketball team repeat its success of the past two years? With high-scoring Vernon Butler gone, opposing teams put two and three men on David. Even so, the team clicked from the start.

David was still rewriting the record book. He became the first college player to score 2,500 points, grab 1,450 rebounds, and shoot over 60 percent from the field. His NCAA record for blocked shots climbed to 516. His miracle half-court shot beat James Madison University. Almost lost in the excitement was the fact that David scored 33 points and snatched 13 rebounds that day.

In January, Secretary of the Navy John F. Lehman, Jr., cut David's active-duty time to two years. David began making plans to play with a pro team in his off-duty hours. Napoleon McCallum, a lieutenant, was already playing football part-time for the Los Angeles Raiders. The news did not please everyone. An Annapolis education costs the taxpayers a ton of money, some argued. Two years, they said, wasn't enough payback.

The debate faded when the NCAA tournament began. The Middies, flying high with a 30–5 record, played Michigan in the first round. The Wolverines held on to win, 97–82, despite David's school-record 50 points. His teammates hugged him when he left the game.

College basketball awards 12 major trophies to its top players. In 1987 David won all 12. Every **All-American** team in the land featured the College Player of the Year at center.

Bad news has a way of following good. The new secretary of the navy, James Webb, ruled that officers could not play part-

The proud recipient of the 1987 Eastman Award for college basketball's Player of the Year, David displays his trophy for photographers.

time for the pros. However, Webb left intact the ruling that reduced David's commitment to two years. Navy ships still lacked headroom for 7-foot officers.

The decision raised new questions. Would a National Basketball Association (NBA) team draft David, knowing he couldn't play for two years? If he was drafted, would he sign? Many people thought he should wait. When he left the Navy, in 1989, he would be a **free agent**. Free agents, they reminded him, can sign with any team they wish.

Top NBA draft choice David Robinson chats with Vice President George Bush during a 1987 visit to the White House.

Chapter 6

Two Years Is a Long Time

In May 1987 the National Basketball Association held its yearly lottery. Top prize was first pick of the nation's college players. The name that dropped out of the hopper read *San Antonio Spurs*. Bob Bass, the team's general manager, was all smiles. "There's no doubt in my mind that we will pick David [Robinson]," he said.

David was too busy to worry about the **pro draft**. Three days after the lottery, the new ensign received his degree. In mid-June he reported for duty at the King's Bay Submarine Base in Georgia. The Navy put him in charge of construction work on the base's docks.

During his stay in southeast Georgia, David witnessed the

effect of prejudice, drugs, and abuse on children. "It was real life," he says. "I had always been judged on my abilities, never on whether I was black or white.…It was all so sad. I got on my knees and asked God to give me a way to give back some of my blessings."

In June the NBA held its regular draft. David was playing golf when he heard that San Antonio had used its lottery pick to draft him. He told reporters that he wasn't sure he would sign with the Spurs. This is a losing team, he said, pointing to the Spurs' 28–54 record.

Late that summer David joined Team U.S.A. for the Pan Am Games. The Americans won their first two contests, but David's play was subpar. He improved at both ends of the court in the semifinal win over Puerto Rico. But hopes of a gold medal vanished in the finals against Brazil. David fouled out late in the fourth quarter. With its big center on the bench, the United States lost the high-scoring game, 120–115.

In September, San Antonio gave David a warm welcome. Bob Bass assured him that the team was committed to winning. He backed up his promise with a $26 million, eight-year offer. Two months later, David signed the contract and put the money in a trust fund. Doing so allowed him to play in the 1988 Olympics as an amateur.

David was rusty, but his raw talent won him a place on the Olympic team. Coach John Thompson told him to play himself into shape. On a tour of Europe, sportswriters and teammates criticized David's play. "I'm only 70 percent of where I want to be," he admitted.

The Americans went to South Korea favored to win Olympic gold. The luck of the draw matched them against the Soviet Union in the semifinals. Behind at halftime, David and his teammates rallied to close the gap to 59–57. At that critical point their shooting went cold. The Soviets ran off with the game, 82–76. The United States went on to take the bronze medal, but no one's heart was in the game.

Team U.S.A.'s David Robinson drives against Spain's Antonio Martin during first-round Olympic basketball action in Seoul, South Korea, in 1988.

David had not played badly. He scored 19 points and grabbed 12 rebounds in his rematch with big Arvidas Sabonis. But pro sports is a world where winning is everything. Doubts arose about David's talent. A two-year layoff, people whispered, is too long. Even his friends wondered whether he could come back.

New York Knicks' Patrick Ewing tries unsuccessfully to block a shot by David in this 1989 game at Madison Square Garden.

Chapter 7

Breaking In with the Pros

David's discharge from the Navy came through in May 1989. He moved to San Antonio and invited Freda and Ambrose to help him settle in. The arrangement worked out so well that David asked his parents to stay in the Texas city. He sealed the deal by buying them a house. He moved into a condo and furnished it with a baby grand piano. It was time to brush up on his music skills, he said. The sounds of Beethoven and other classical composers soon filled his home.

While David sharpened his game in a summer pro league, his team was being rebuilt. The Spurs added Terry Cummings, Maurice Cheeks, and **rookie** Sean Elliott to their lineup. Even so, new head coach Larry Brown was growing impatient. Brown had just suffered through his first losing season, 21–61. "If David hadn't been here, I wouldn't have come," he said.

In October 1989, David reported to training camp. His weight was up to 235 and he was bench-pressing 200 pounds. He looked like his old self in preseason games, but the real test came in November. In his first regular season pro game, David faced Magic Johnson and the Los Angeles Lakers. Two minutes into the game, he threw in a perfect reverse slam dunk. From there he went on to score 23 points and collect 17 rebounds. After the Spurs' 106–98 win, Magic talked about David's play. "He's a man already, you know," he said. "Some guys just aren't ever rookies."

The Spurs roared through the first part of the season. On January 16, 1990, in a game against the Knicks, David scored 20 points, grabbed 12 rebounds, and blocked 4 shots. With 1:27 left in the game, Knicks center Patrick Ewing tied the score on a **layup**. Sixteen seconds later, David hit a turnaround jumper. From there the lead seesawed back and forth. With only 16 seconds left, Ewing tried to muscle his way to the basket. David timed his leap perfectly and blocked the shot. His clutch play saved the game.

Sportswriters who once said David would flop in the pros now sang his praises. He was named Rookie of the Month six times and Player of the Week three times. The nation's fans called him the Admiral and put him on the All-Star team. Matched against the NBA's top stars, David scored 15 points and pulled in 10 rebounds.

On road trips the team bus often left without him. David stayed behind to give interviews and sign autographs. Fans admired his basketball skills and his clean, drug-free life. Look, they said, the Admiral stands at attention for the national anthem. Nike featured him in its ads. David played the role of a children's TV host in *Mr. Robinson's Neighborhood*. His message downplayed shoe sales in favor of asking kids to stay off drugs.

Number 50 was the league's second best rebounder, but Coach Brown thought he lacked intensity. The coach couldn't fault the Spurs' record, however. The team went 56–26, clinching the division title on the last day of the regular season. The 35-game turnaround set an NBA record for improvement from one year to the next. Naturally, David was voted Rookie of the Year. His 24.3 points, 12 rebounds, and 3.89 blocks per game earned him the honor.

The Spurs opened the play-offs against the Denver Nuggets. After sweeping the Nuggets in three straight, they moved on to play the Portland Trail Blazers. The teams split the first six games. The seventh game went into overtime before the Blazers pulled out a win. Portland went on to the NBA finals, and the Spurs went home.

Chapter 8

Building a New Life

David reported for **naval reserve** training each summer. After playing 80-plus games a season, he found the two weeks of active duty a welcome change. When the 1990–1991 season rolled around, the Admiral went back to work. He soon proved that his rookie success had not been a fluke. On offense he averaged 25.6 points a game. At the defensive end he led the NBA with 320 blocks and 1,063 rebounds. Fans rewarded his sparkling play by making him a starter in the All-Star game.

The Gulf War broke out early in 1991. Many of David's academy classmates were risking their lives in the Persian Gulf. In a *Sports Illustrated* interview, David said, "It was pretty intense for me. I turned on the news, and the announcer said the

*David drives the baseline and leads the Spurs to a 96-95
victory over the Houston Rockets.*

guys on the first planes had left that morning for a bombing run over Baghdad....That made playing basketball seem insignificant."

War or no war, basketball-mad fans filled San Antonio's HemisFair Arena night after night. The Spurs responded by winning 55 games and a second straight Midwest Division title. Every team starts over again in the play-offs, however. David's 25.8 points a game were not enough to beat the hot-shooting Golden State Warriors. The unexpected loss ended the year on a sour note.

In 1991–1992, the Spurs seemed ready to compete for an NBA title. Then the team hit a run of bad luck. Coach Brown quit in January 1992, leaving general manager Bob Bass to fill in for him. Willie Anderson played much of the season with a stress fracture. Terry Cummings, David's best friend, missed 12 games. The final blow came on March 16. David tore the ligaments in his left thumb in a game against the Charlotte Hornets. Although he tried to play with his hand in a splint, the pain was too great. A surgeon repaired the damage, but David did not play again that season. The Spurs sagged without him and finished second, eight games behind Utah.

Even though he sat out 14 games, David's 305 blocked shots led the NBA. Eleven of those blocks came in one game against Portland. Thanks in large part to David's defense, the Blazers made only one **field goal** in the last four minutes. The play-offs were another matter. Forced to play without their leader, the Spurs lost three straight games to Phoenix.

The 1991–1992 season did have some high points. During the summer of 1991, David had worked hard at conquering what he called his spiritual "imperfections." Then, on the morning of December 17, he married Valerie Hoggatt. Instead of leaving for a honeymoon, David left that afternoon to play in Dallas. Perhaps he wanted to give his new wife a wedding present. The Admiral chalked up 22 points, 12 rebounds, and 8 blocks in a 98–87 victory.

Coach Pat Riley of the Knicks said David was better than Hall of Famer Bill Russell. Like Russell, he was a tower of strength on defense. Before David came along, no other player had ranked in the top five in rebounds, blocked shots, and steals. Jack Sikma, the Milwaukee center, marveled at his quickness and leaping ability. "It's unfair, that's what it is," he joked.

As his hand healed, David looked ahead to the 1992 Olympic Games. Playing for the **Dream Team** would give him a second chance at a gold medal.

Two points for the Dream Team as David dunks the ball during this 1992 Olympic game against Brazil.

Chapter 9

Good as Gold

Nobody called it the 1992 U.S. Olympic basketball team. Wherever basketball was played, this was the Dream Team. Fans around the globe said it was the best team ever assembled.

In other years pros had been barred from playing Olympic basketball. Now, for the first time, the International Basketball Federation (FIBA) asked the United States to send its best players. FIBA's Boris Stankovic explained, "Only [by] playing against the best teams can people improve."

The Dream Team roster read like a *Who's Who* of the NBA:
Charles Barkley, forward, Phoenix Suns
Larry Bird, forward, Boston Celtics

Clyde Drexler, guard, Portland Trail Blazers
Patrick Ewing, center, New York Knicks
Magic Johnson, guard, Los Angeles Lakers
Michael Jordan, guard, Chicago Bulls
Christian Laettner, forward, Duke University/
   Minnesota Timberwolves
Karl Malone, forward, Utah Jazz
Chris Mullin, forward, Golden State Warriors
Scottie Pippen, forward, Chicago Bulls
David Robinson, center, San Antonio Spurs
John Stockton, guard, Utah Jazz
Coach Chuck Daly, New Jersey Nets

Bill Wennington, a center for Canada, played against the United States in a regional tournament. The Dream Team stomped all over his team and five other opponents. Afterward, Wennington declared, "The world will end before the United States is beaten."

The prediction was right on target. David and his teammates won all 14 of their games by an average score of 122–72. Opposing teams treated the lopsided losses as badges of honor. Brazil, long an Olympic basketball power, lost by 44 points. Oscar Schmidt, the team's star, told the press, "I loved it. They are my idols. I will remember this game for the rest of my life."

Minor injuries slowed David, Stockton, Ewing, Drexler, and Pippen. Bird's painful back cut down his playing time. But, as Pippen said, "We could probably win the gold with five guys." Magic Johnson, making a comeback after being diagnosed as having HIV, the virus that causes AIDS, explained it this way: "On your regular team, when you're running a fast break, you're always thinking...'I can't give it to *him*.' On this team, you can give it to *anybody*."

The Dream Teamers won their first seven games at Barcelona. The win streak set up a gold medal match against Croatia. The Croatians were flying high after beating the **Unified Team**. Their happy fans held up signs that read, "America Next!"

The game started like most of the others. Magic passed to Jordan, who swished a jumper. Ewing grabbed an offensive rebound and hooked it in. But Croatia, led by Toni Kukoc, fought back. Midway through the first half, the underdog Croatians took the lead, 25–23. At that point the Dream Team turned on the power. Shooting an incredible 67 percent from the field, the United States coasted to a 117–85 victory. David did his share with 9 points and 3 blocked shots.

At the gold medal ceremony, he let Magic do the talking. "It's the most awesome feeling I've ever had winning anything," Magic said. "I've got goose bumps all over my body."

Chapter 10

A New Leadership Role

The Spurs faced a big adjustment going into the 1992–1993 season. Recently hired head coach Jerry ("Tark") Tarkanian was new to pro ball. The opening game showed that the college veteran had much to learn. When the Admiral took a hard fall, Tark didn't know how to call for a 20-second time-out. Despite the problems, David refused to bad-mouth his coach. "He can flat-out coach," he said. "He's very good at showing he cares."

Troubled by health problems, Tark continued to flounder. The fans began to complain as the Spurs staggered to a 9–11 start. On December 18, 1992, owner Red McCombs fired the coach he had hired with so much fanfare. Then he surprised everyone by hiring John ("Luke") Lucas to take his place.

David tries to block a shot by Hakeem Olajuwon of the Rockets during the first period of this 1992 game in Houston.

Lucas was a story all by himself. First, he was an African American in a league whose coaches are mostly white. Second, he was a former pro star whose career had been cut short by cocaine. After kicking drugs, Luke started a detox clinic for athletes with similar problems. Lloyd Daniels of the Spurs was only one of the basketball players he had helped. Third, Luke was untested as a coach. His only coaching experience had been with his own minor league team.

Convinced that the players were out of shape, Luke drove them hard. Panting hard after his first workout under Luke's coaching, David had to agree. In one killer drill, the team was given one minute to run sideline to sideline 17 times.

The Spurs won their first game with Luke and picked up speed from there. In their next 26 games they lost only 3. Luke put new life into the Spurs' running game. To take advantage of the Admiral's **inside game**, he designed a new half-court offense.

Luke often let the players make the decisions. He also asked David to take a more active role as team captain. The former Navy officer agreed. "I've always wanted to be involved, but no one was interested in what I had to say," he told a reporter.

The low-key coach can—and does—yell at his players. "Sometimes…he'll yell, 'You're not giving us anything!'" David explained. "Some coaches say stuff like that, you…don't even listen. With John, we listen. He's bringing our heads and our hearts together."

The "new" Spurs sometimes looked unreal. In a home game against the L.A. Clippers, they raced off to an early lead. Instead of relaxing, they stretched it to 13 by halftime and 17 by the third quarter. David put in a typical "day at the office." He scored 25 points, pulled down 13 rebounds, and blocked 7 shots. On January 16, 1993, he exploded for a career-high 52 points against the Charlotte Hornets. Fans voted him to the All-Star team for the fourth time in four years.

On March 30 the Spurs clinched a play-off berth, but the magic was wearing thin. The defense sagged and the team's scoring average dropped. Houston pulled ahead in the race for the Midwest Division title. Through all the ups and downs, David played his usual strong game. He ranked in the NBA's top ten in scoring, rebounding, and shot blocking.

The Spurs pulled themselves together for the play-offs. With David scoring well and raking in the rebounds, they beat Portland in the first round. The upset win sent them to Phoenix to play Charles Barkley and the heavily favored Suns. With Phoenix leading 3–2 in games, the series came down to a one-on-one play between two superstars. The score was tied and only seconds remained when Barkley faked a drive to the basket. The fake gave him room to swish a jumpshot over David's upstretched fingers.

The Spurs tried to set David up for a last-second shot, but his desperation attempt was blocked. San Antonio's strange and wonderful roller-coaster season was over.

David joins with other famous athletes to record a song written to help young people make wise decisions about sexual behavior. From left to right: Darryl Green of the Washington Redskins, Barry Sanders of the Detroit Lions, David Robinson, and A. C. Green of the Los Angeles Lakers.

Chapter 11

"A Tremendous Human Being"

David Robinson is much more than a superb athlete. His intelligence, wit, and life-style stand out among pro superstars. At each home game he provides free seats to *Mr. Robinson's Neighborhood* for 50 high-achieving students. David also adopted 90 fifth graders through the "I Have a Dream" Foundation. Thanks to the Admiral, each student who goes on to college will receive a $2,300 scholarship. The gift greatly impressed the foundation's chairperson. "David Robinson is a tremendous human being," Marie Goforth says.

With an income of over $5 million a year, the Admiral can afford to be generous. He could make more money, but he refuses to sign **endorsement contracts** for products that don't fit his clean-cut image. Nike's ads fit that image perfectly. Instead of relying totally on an agent, he lets the Robinson Group handle his money, public appearances, and charity work. David's parents and cousin Aldrich Mitchell serve as the group's chief officers.

Basketball pays the bills, but sports are not an obsession with David. His home life revolves around Valerie and their son, David, Jr. He likes to relax with friends on the golf course or at a bowling alley. On road trips, he works on logic puzzles, reads science fiction, and practices the saxophone. During the Olympics he sat in on a rooftop jam session with Branford Marsalis. Now he jokes about "jamming with President [Bill] Clinton," another amateur sax player.

David's coaches say that he was born with a handicap—too much brain. He drives them crazy when he "spaces out" in the middle of a game. During these "walkabouts" he's probably thinking about the new song he is writing or a computer problem. A slam dunk by an opposing center usually brings him back.

The walkabouts come less often these days. A 1993 poll ranked him as the NBA's best center. *Inside Sports* magazine's total individual performance (TIP) analysis confirmed the rating. TIP calculates the number of games a team would lose if a star is replaced by an average player. David's TIP of 15.39 means that without him the Spurs would have lost 15 more games. Only Michael Jordan, with a TIP of 17.96, ranked higher. The next closest center is Ewing, at 12.97.

The scary thing about David, opponents say, is that he is still improving. Sportswriters have already labeled him as a sure bet for the Hall of Fame. All he has to do is keep his mind on the game.

More Good Reading About David Robinson

If you want to read more about David, look for these two books: Dawn Miller's *David Robinson, Backboard Admiral* (Minneapolis: Lerner Publications, 1991) and John Rolfe's *David Robinson* (Boston: Little, Brown, 1991). Both books describe David's life and career through his 1990-1991 season with the Spurs. After that you'll have to dig for articles in magazines and newspapers.

Sports Illustrated (November 19, 1986): Curry Kirkpatrick—"The Mightiest Middie"; (April 22, 1991): Bruce Newman—"Horn of Plenty"; (March 2, 1992): Rick Telander—"They Could Use a Spur"

Sporting News (April 23, 1990): Paul Attner—"Well Worth the Wait"

GQ (February 1991): Pat Jordan—"King David"

Playboy (June 1991): Jeff Coplon—"Air Apparent"

Los Angeles Times Magazine (March 22, 1992): Edward Kiersh—"Mr. Robinson vs. Air Jordan"

FIBA Basketball Monthly (February 1993): "Here's to You, Mr. Robinson"

Newsmakers: The People Behind Today's Headlines (Detroit: Gale Research, 1992). Pages 392–395

Glossary

All-American   An honorary team made up of the nation's best college players in a particular sport. All-American teams are picked by sportswriters, coaches, and sports foundations.

blocked shot   A play in which a defender prevents a possible basket by knocking away an attempted shot.

Dream Team   The nickname given to the U.S. basketball team that played in the 1992 Summer Olympics in Spain.

endorsement contract   An agreement in which popular athletes are paid to serve as spokespersons for a company's products.

field goal   Any successful two-point or three-point shot taken from the floor during a basketball game.

foul out   To commit a fifth foul (college) or a sixth foul (pro ball), which requires the offending player to leave the game.

free agent   A professional player in any sport who can sign with any team he or she chooses.

inside game   An offensive strategy that calls for the players to work the ball close to the basket before attempting a shot.

layup   A field goal scored from a spot close to the basket.

NCAA tournament   A series of play-off games organized by the National Collegiate Athletic Association to determine the champion team in basketball.

naval reserve   Inactive Navy personnel who can be called back to active duty in the event of war or other national emergency.

plebe   Name given to first-year students at the U.S. Naval Academy.

pro draft   A system by which pro teams take turns picking the top college stars from each year's crop of eligible players. The teams with the worst records draft ahead of the better teams. The highly prized first pick in the draft is determined by a lottery system.

rebound   The act of jumping to catch a missed shot after it bounces off the rim or backboard.

rookie   An athlete playing for the first time at a more advanced level.

slam dunk   An impossible-to-stop scoring play in which the player jumps high enough to stuff the ball through the basket from above it.

steal   The act of taking the ball away from the offensive team.

three-point shot   A field goal scored from beyond the 19 foot 9 inch line (college) or the 23 foot 9 inch line (pro ball). It counts as three points. Field goals scored from inside the three-point line count as two points.

triple-double   A rare achievement in which a player attains double figures in three of four important statistics: scoring, rebounding, assists, and blocked shots.

Unified Team   The name given to an athletic team from countries that once belonged to the Soviet Union.

INDEX